ABC

of
Australian
and
African Animals

By Pene and John Cleaves

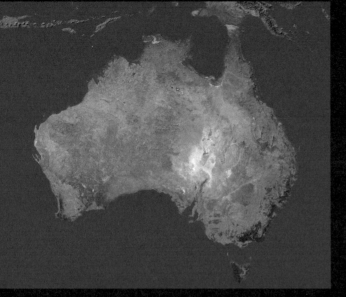

Australia

Azure Kingfisher

Africa

Aardvark

African Antelope

African Wild Cat

African Wild Dog

Bee-Eater

Blue Winged Kooraburra

Brown Eagle

Baboons

Black Rhinoceros

Brownheaded Kingfisher

Bearded Dragon

Black Breasted Buzzard

Bug

Bandicoot

Bushbuck

Bats

Blister Beetle

Butterfly

Barn Owl

Bustard

Brolga

Blue Tongue Lizard

Black Swan

Blue Billed Duck

Blue Wildebeest

Bushbaby

Cheetah

Curlew

Childrens Python

Cormorant

Cassowary

Chicken

Common Eland

Crocodile

Camel

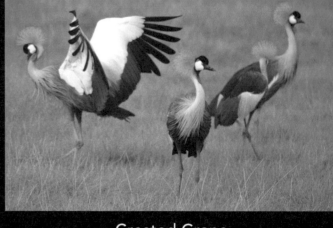

Crested Crane

Caracal

Cockatiel

Cape Buffalo

Dog

Dikdik

Donkey

Dragonfly

Dung Beetle

Dingo

Duck

Dolphin

Elephant Female with Babies

Elephant Male

Echidna

Eagle

Egret

Flamingo

Fur Seal

Go Away Bird

Glossy Starling

Frogmouth Owl

Grants Gazelle

Grey Duiker

Giant Plated Lizard

Giant Kingfisher

Giraffe

Goat

Galah

Gecko

Goose

Grasshopper

Green Tree Frog

Guinea Fowl

Goanna

Honeyeater

Hyena

Heron Goliath

Honey Badger

Hammerhead

Horse

Hippopotamus

Hartebeest

Hyrax

Impala Female

Jackal

Impala Male

Jabiru

Kangaroo

Kestrel

Koala

Kudu Female

Leopard Tortoise

Kudu Male

Kookaburra

Lilac Breasted Roller

Lion

Lioness

Lion Cubs

Leopard

Lizard

Lorikeets

Little Penguin

Meercat

Magpie

Mongoose

Monkey Blue

Mouse

Marabou Stork

Murray Darling Python

Numbat

Nyala Female

Nyala Male

Owl Tawny

Ostrich Female

Ostrich Male

Pigeon

Parrot

Platypus

Peacock

Pelican

Possum

Porcupine

Quail

Quokka

Quoll

Rhinoceros White

Red Duiker

Red Billed Hornbill

Rock Wallaby

Rabbit

Rosella

Rail Buff Banded

Red and Yellow Tailed Cockatoo

Red Kangaroo

Scops Owl   Southern BooBook Owl   Southern Ground Hornbill

Sea Eagle   Serval

Stork   Steinbuck

Secretary Bird

Sunburst Starling

Squirrel

Snake

Sea-lion

Spider

Sulphur Crested Cockatoo

Stumpy Lizard

Turtle

Tasmanian Devil

Thompsons Gazelle

Tsessebe

Us Under Umbrella Thorn Tree

Vervet Monkey

Violet Backed Starling

Vultures

Warthog Family

Warthog Male

Waterbuck

Wombat

Wedge Tailed Eagle

Weaver

White Tailed Mongoose

Yellow Weaver

Y Bug

Xyris

Yellow Billed Hornbill

Yellow Bearded Wildebeest

Zebra Baby

Zebra

Zebra Herd

Balboa Press books may be ordered through booksellers or by contacting:

Balboa Press
A Division of Hay House
1663 Liberty Drive
Bloomington, IN 47403
www.balboapress.com.au
1 (877) 407-4847

Because of the dynamic nature of the Internet, any web addresses or links contained in this book may have changed since publication and may no longer be valid. The views expressed in this work are solely those of the author and do not necessarily reflect the views of the publisher, and the publisher hereby disclaims any responsibility for them.

Any people depicted in stock imagery provided by Getty Images are models, and such images are being used for illustrative purposes only.
Certain stock imagery © Getty Images.

ISBN: 978-1-5043-1734-4 (sc)
ISBN: 978-1-5043-1733-7 (e)

Print information available on the last page.

Balboa Press rev. date: 04/11/2019

BALBOA.
PRESS
A DIVISION OF HAY HOUSE

Printed in the United States
By Bookmasters